# SPEAK YOUR TRUTH

# Also by Mariëlle S. Smith

*52 Weeks of Writing Author Journal and Planner, Vol. I: Get out of your own way and become the writer you're meant to be*

*52 Weeks of Writing Author Journal and Planner, Vol. II: Get out of your own way and become the writer you're meant to be*

*52 Weeks of Writing Author Journal and Planner, Vol. III: Get out of your own way and become the writer you're meant to be*

*365 Days of Gratitude Journal: Commit to the life-changing power of gratitude by creating a sustainable practice*

*365 Days of Gratitude Journal, Vol. II: Commit to the life-changing power of gratitude by creating a sustainable practice*

*Fleshing Out the Narrative: A 31-Day Tarot and Journal Challenge for Writers*

*Get Out of Your Own Way: A 31-Day Tarot Challenge for Writers and Other Creatives*

*Set Yourself Up for Success: A 31-Day Tarot Challenge for Writers and Other Creatives*

*Seven Simple Spreads 1: Seven Simple Card Spreads to Unlock Your Creative Flow*

*Seven Simple Spreads 2: Seven Simple Card Spreads to Direct Your Creative Flow*

*Seven Simple Spreads 3: Seven Simple Card Spreads to Boost Your Confidence*

*Seven Simple Spreads 4: Seven Simple Card Spreads to Celebrate Your Creative Wins*

*Step into Your Power: A 31-Day Tarot Challenge to Unleash Your Creative Potential*

*Tarot for Creatives: 21 Tarot Spreads to (Re)Connect to Your Intuition and Ignite that Creative Spark*

# Co-written under the pen name Heather MacLee

*Too Good to Be True?*

*Where There's a Will*

*There's a Way*

# Speak Your Truth

**A 31-day tarot challenge**
for writers and other creatives

**Mariëlle S. Smith**

ISBN 978 94 93250 04 8

For Andri, who hears me always

# INTRODUCTION

Welcome to *Speak Your Truth*, a 31-day tarot challenge for writers and other creatives. It means everything to me that you're here, because it means you're ready to say what you have to say.

And we need more of those in the world, especially now.

The thirty-one daily prompts in this book will help you *uncover* your truth, *understand* what's been blocking it, and *unlearn* the behaviours that have kept you from speaking up. They will make you reflect on:

- who you were before your voice became blocked,
- what is stopping your from speaking your truth(s),
- how you not speaking up has both limited and served you,
- how you not speaking up has both limited and served others, and
- who you could be once you embrace your truth(s) fully,

all the while preparing you to start taking actual steps towards speaking your truth.

## Doing a tarot challenge

How does a tarot challenge work? Quite simply. Each day, you pick up your deck of choice, shuffle to your heart's content, and pick a card or more, depending on the question and what your gut tells you. The next day, you put the card(s) back into your deck, shuffle like you mean it, and pull out your next draw.

I only suggest the number of cards you could be drawing on occasion, but you should feel absolutely free to draw as many as you like no matter what day or question. Your gut always knows best. Likewise, it doesn't matter how you shuffle your cards or decide which card is the one that needs picking. Just go with what you've been taught or feels right for you in this moment. There's really no doing this wrong.

The same goes with how you interpret the cards' messages. Some feel utterly comfortable using the guidebook that came with their deck, while others rely solely on their intuition. You can do either or a bit of both: when doing a reading, I don't mind glancing at the description offered by the creator of the cards, especially when I feel there is more to a card but I just can't seem to grasp the full meaning of it at the time. The guidebook won't always bridge that gap, but it might just give you another perspective, that 'Aha, of course!' moment that will kickstart your intuition. Whatever you do, don't let others tell you what is right and wrong: there's only a right and wrong for you, and you will know what is what in the moment.

I highly suggest that you write down your findings and reflect on them as you go. The same card might show up again and again: what could that mean? Some cards will only make sense later, after you answer a few more questions. Reflecting on previous draws will be especially relevant in those cases. And, even if all the cards make perfect sense the moment you draw them, looking at the bigger picture might still reveal something you hadn't considered before. It's in the reflecting that the wisdom lies.

Use whatever works for you

Those familiar with my work know that I don't differentiate between means of divination. I might use the word tarot, but you can use any deck of cards, whether that be tarot, oracle, or angel. If you'd rather use your crystals or your runes, feel free to go with that.

For those who want to do the challenge but aren't comfortable using either of those divinatory tools, or simply don't own any, use each question as a journal prompt. Sit down in a quiet space, take a few deep breaths, and let whatever answers need to bubble to the surface come.

Likewise, if you would like to mix things up—perhaps the one question makes you want to grab your favourite oracle deck, while another makes you pick up a notebook—please do. Your challenge, your rules. As long as you follow that gut of yours.

What does speaking my own truth mean to me?

Draw one or two cards.

How have I been speaking my truth?

Take a look at some of your previous work. Single out two to three projects that you feel capture your true voice. If you don't feel any of them do, choose those that come closest.

Now, for every project you picked, draw a card with the question in mind.

What truth have I been yearning to speak?

Why has the time come for me to speak this truth?

# DAY 5

What has kept me from speaking this truth before?

Today, look at the pile of work you've never finished or shown to anyone. Pick two or three pieces you felt especially passionate about when you first started working on it. Before you draw any cards, sit with these pieces for some time. Ask yourself why you've never finished them and write down your answer.

Now, for every answer you wrote down, draw a card and reflect. What do the cards have to say about your reasoning?

# DAY 6

What is blocking me from speaking my truth now?

When was this block created?

Blocks aren't created all at once. The initial seed sown grows into a block over time, as it is triggered by new events. Draw as many cards as you need to determine how your block as developed.

If you have any energy left after this exercise, try to sit with who was involved in this development. Who do you see through the cards that showed up? Whose voice(s) do you hear?

How have I allowed this block to take my voice away?

Why have I allowed this block to take my voice away?

Who was I before this block impacted on my life?

Think of the last time you felt fully free to express your authentic self. What is the first thing that comes to mind? What do you see when going back to that version of yourself? Write it down.

Now, draw a card a card to reflect on the you that was. What is it you need to remember right now?

How has this block limited me?

Draw three cards. Before you turn them over, think of a moment in your life when your inability to speak your truth was palpable. Write down what happend and how it made you feel.

Now, turn the three cards over and reflect.

How has this block served me?

Make a list of all the ways in which your inability to speak your truth has served your ego, that part of you that is determined to keep yourself safe and small at all costs.

Now, draw two cards as you ask yourself the question and reflect.

How has this block limited others?

When we don't speak our truths, others might not feel the freedom to speak theirs. Draw at least one card to reflect on how your being blocked is a disservice to others.

How has this block served others?

Think back to two or three moments in your life when you holding your tongue served the purpose of others.

Draw a card for each moment and reflect.

# DAY 15

What part of me is still holding on to this block?

Where does my truth spring from?

Draw as many cards as you like.

# DAY 17

Why am I the one to have to speak this truth?

# DAY 18

What is it about this truth that makes me afraid to raise my voice, or even open my mouth?

Think of a moment in the past when you did speak your truth, but the response wasn't what you hoped for.

Draw one or more cards, asking: What does my truth want me to know about this event?

# DAY 20

Who could I become once I fully gain my voice back and start speaking my truth for real?

# DAY 21

Think of two to three truth speakers you admire.

What is it that you admire about the way these people use their voices? Write it down.

When you're done, draw a card for each truth speaker and reflect.

Go back to the truth speakers you chose yesterday.

Think of a moment in time when they were under attack for what they'd said. Reflect on how they dealt with that situation.

Then, draw a card for each, asking: What lesson can I draw from this truth speaker right now?

Think of one thing you could do today to start speaking your truth. It doesn't have to be a major leap! Unlearning takes time and dedicated effort.

Once you figured out what is in reach for you today, draw a card and reflect on its advice. When you're ready, go take that step.

I'm not kidding, go do it!

# DAY 24

Let's return to the step you took yesterday.
How are you feeling about it now?

Draw a card, asking yourself: What do I need
to know about the step taken yesterday?

What other steps must I take to free my voice
and start speaking my truth?

Draw as many cards as necessary.

# DAY 26

Draw a card for each step you singled out yesterday, asking: What advice about this step do I need to embrace?

Look at your past work. Knowing what you know now, pick one project that you would love to finish or put out there after all.

Draw a card, asking: What do I have to keep in mind as I finally bring this work to completion/out into the world?

Now, look at the project you're currently
working on.

Draw two cards, asking: What do I have to
remember about my truth as I bring this
work to completion/out into the world?

What do I know now that my old self didn't?

Draw two cards.

Now I know this (card 1) about my truth, I will
remember to do (card 2) whenever I'm afraid
to speak up.

Draw one or two final cards. Use the (combined) message to create a personal mantra for the future.

Once you're done, I invite you to take a sheet of paper and write your truth-speaking mantra down. If you'd rather paint or embroider it, go right ahead.

Now hang it in a spot where you can see it as you work. If you feel like sharing, take a picture and send it to *marielle@mswordsmith.nl*. I'd love to see what you come up with.

# Please Consider Leaving a Review

Authors are nowhere without honest reviews, and I'd truly appreciate it if you left one on Goodreads, my Facebook page facebook.com/mswordsmith, or the retailer where you bought this book.

# The Creative Cardslingers

## Isn't it better to sling cards together?

Join my private Facebook group The Creative Cardslingers (password **LAPIS LAZULI**) to meet fellow creative cardreaders, be the first to test my latest card spreads, and hear all about the creative projects I'm involved in.

# Want More?

Head over to mswordsmith.nl/starterkit and get my free Get Out of Your Own Way Starter Kit now.

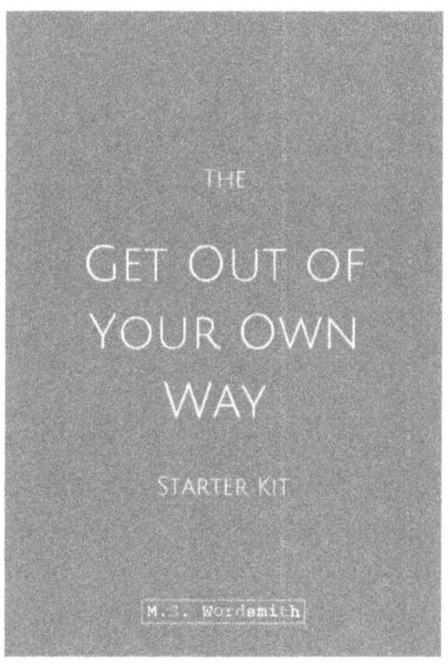

The Get Out of Your Own Way Starter Kit includes four different tools:

- An exercise on limiting beliefs,
- a monthly tracking and reflecting worksheet,
- a meditation on letting go of limiting beliefs,
- a tarot spread on creative roadblocks (from *Tarot for Creatives*),

and is yours when signing up to my newsletter.

# ABOUT ME

I'm a coach for writers and other creatives, an editor, a writer, an intuitive healer, and a custom retreat organiser. Born in the Netherlands and raised by my Dutch mother and Scottish expat father, I moved to the island of Cyprus in February 2019.

The thing about being somewhere new is that it sheds a different light on your life. Your mind opens up to other perspectives, and you find yourself brimming with new ideas. Or old ideas you never wanted to take seriously suddenly demand your attention.

Bringing the spiritual into my work was a scary step for me, because I've always tried to keep the two separate. I say 'tried' because quite a few of my clients, and the work they brought with them, have forced me to merge my professional background with my spiritual interests. Some hired me to edit or translate their holistic books, others came to me for coaching and were struggling in a way that needed a broader approach. And then there are the many writers and other creatives who are openly incorporating spirituality into their practice as we speak.

Over the past year, I've switched gears and gradually allowed the spiritual to enter my workspace. This book is one of its many manifestations. It goes without saying that I hope you'll enjoy it, and get from it everything you need.

**Want to get in touch? There are different ways and places to contact me:**

Website: mswordsmith.nl
E-mail: marielle@mswordsmith.nl
instagram.com/mariellessmith
facebook.com/mswordsmith

# ACKNOWLEDGEMENTS

I couldn't have done this without my
fellow creative cardslingers.

I owe you everything.

www.ingramcontent.com/pod-product-compliance
Lightning Source LLC
Chambersburg PA
CBHW071254130726
47998CB00003B/1180